Apricity

R. C. Cannady

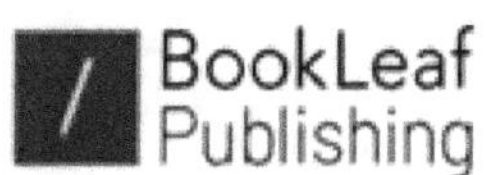

Presentation by *BookLeaf Publishing*

Web: www.bookleafpub.com

E-mail: info@bookleafpub.com

ISBN: 9789358312003

First edition 2022

Love me Knots

I stepped on a petal.
What an immeasurable death!
A beauteous forever,
Exhaled in one perfumed breath.

I felt a crushed heart beneath irresponsible step,
And I trembled a bit as, up, her memory crept.

Engulfing the caverns, up in to my brain-
This soft little soul- it punctured a vein.

My mind opened up, and it hurt to remember,
That the loveliest of Earth's aroma
Will be destroyed in November.

So as a final Spring thought performed behind
my eyes-
I picked up the petal, and I blew it aside.

How it Ends for You

How it ends for you:

This is how it ends for you.
The silence is deafening as you wake up again-
2pm
Your olfactory sense fails you-
Again.
You push the litter of processed cheese crumbs
and rotting chicken flesh under the pillow and sit
up
'BLURRY'
"Could one of these cans have some left?"
You frivolously collect the few ethanol drops.
It's not enough.
It's never enough.
Somehow your cheek feels the pillow again.
No more adderall.
Back to sleep.
There's a knock at the door
-but you'd never know.
They've been knocking for 20 minutes
You remember they seem loud.
Back to sleep.
You haven't dreamt in years-

It's just blackness.
The Unapologetic Nothing.

It's cold. Why is it so cold?
Eyes closed, you reach-
Reach for the bedside table
-Not knowing what for.

Nothing.

There's no table.
You've reached far enough to fall off of the steel
slab.
Later you hear the story
Of how you resisted arrest-
And spit
And cursed
And bled from the wrists
In an attempt to free yourself
From the bonds of cold, silver society
Taking its revenge on you.
One of these days
You'll contemplate suicide
But remember your cowardice.

Back to sleep.

Did you know

Did you know that zours are discontinued-

- That when I walk in a grocery store, I'm repulsed

Did you know that the tips of stars are the tips of baby fingers
- touching the spaces between our hands and our arms so that we may wave hello and goodbye

Did you know that clouds have always been mashed potatoes?
- Oh woman, you should've guessed by how delicious or disgusting the holidays feel

Did you know that money really does bring happiness?
- A Gucci blanket is always warmer than a bargain.

Did you know I've always wanted to Jill myself?
- Jack and jill go up the hill to fetch a pail of water. They both fell down and broke their

crowns and realized they had to live 89 more
years at the bottom of the hill.

-

The Dipsomaniac Bluffs

The mountains look like bottles-
You hair, it smells like gin-
Or could it be the breath I left to scapegoat my
own sin?

The mounts look like bottles
Who have wilted with you echo-
Three fingers above the rocks and speculation
among tobacco

The mountains look like bottles
-A translucent way to stare.
The last sip has been gone awhile
Why am I still here?

Lush

Well met were we -
Unconsciously
By an Elizabethan Chickadee.

It was far past dawn when I awoke
To hear her speaking Othello's notes.

I felt you ask politely –
If your heavy hand could stay,
Concluding the thought that touch
Could keep today away.

My eyes stumbled toward the window –
And through the eastern air;
Thinking the universe a companion,
For it chose to put me there.

I turned at last to see you,
Still a child of last night;
A conscience in review
Of dormancy's insight.

I thought for a moment to wake you –
But that moment quickly passed,

As I remembered the reason art
Is often veiled with glass.

Act 3, scene 3; I'm grateful it existed.
If not for her, it's safe to say,
I surely would have missed it.

"For she had eyes, and [she] chose me."
Resounded our Elizabethan Chickadee.

Chapter 1: The Great Hate

It was the end.

Not the end of everything, but the end of you.

I sat in the snow-
-Before I had ever enjoyed sitting in the snow.

I let time pass,
Slowly.

And began to write out all our stories.

- The stories that are perpetually imprisoned
in the dusty folds of both our memories.

It was the end.

Not the end of everything, but the end of us.

I sat in the snow –

I hated it.

And then I wrote our book.

Walden

In Concord, Massachusetts,
I skipped around
My sea -

On rocks that
Travelers, I pretended,
Only left for me.

The snow dropped very
Lightly,
And smoke fell
From my mouth

-         In billows

I flicked my imaginary cigarette
And laughed

-         Until

The mountains laughed back at me.

Through the forests,
I cracked each leaf beneath my feet.

Who cares?
They are already dead and gone

But I,
Oh, I am breathing.

And it is cold.

What I Would Have Done

I would've found you one day with my bags
packed.

-Otis' rough paws trailing fervently behind me.

There would've been a confetti-pink flush to my
cheeks

-when I told you that I decided I didn't want to
leave.

I would have been smiling.

I would've sat nervously in the driver's seat on
my way home-

wondering if I'd be good enough for you.

I would've cried that night for fear that I wasn't.

But I would've woken up
Eventually.

And I would have gone through the days with
you.

I would have walked miles with you through the
sun-

-and ran miles with you back to our car in the
rain.

I would have tried to cook.

I would've messed up our meals a million times-

And I would've gotten sensitive about you being
too truthful.

I would have made you coffee.

-And sat with you while you woke up for the
day.

I would have cried at the sad movies we'd watch
-and lie on your shoulder until logic found me
again.

I would have listened to all your bad days at
work
-even if I didn't understand them.

And I would've have gotten you cookies for
all the other things in life I couldn't fix for you.

I would have bought us a house
someday.

And I would have surprised you with a neutral
colored front door.

I would've left you alone to write
-and always wonder if I'd ever been your muse.

I would have pushed you to try harder at the
things you rarely slack on.

I would have fought with you.

And I would have forgiven.

-And asked for forgiveness.

I would've had a son for you.

And everyday I would've told him how beautiful
you are.

I wouldn't have to teach him how to love you
-but I would've taught him why I did.

I would've shown him the magnolias,

the sunshine,

the faint green light at the end of your dock,

the best tasting candy

- and I would've said, "that's dad to me."
And he would understand.

-

I would've bought you a rocking chair too.

And we could've listened to the red birds again.

I would've wondered if we'd ever be cardinals
some day.

And we would've talked for awhile about who
we'd visit when the time came.

-

I would have been frustrating a lot of times
throughout our lives.

But I would have always made sure you were
happy.

I would have gotten sad and
needed to be alone for a while.

-Leaving you to feel like you couldn't help me.

But once the darkness lifted,
And it always would have,
-I would've come back to you whole.

I would have loved you in every way
someone could love another person.

For no other reason than the fact that you are my
friend;
my confidant.
my ride to the airport

I would've loved you as intensely as I do today

-for every other day we had left in this universe.

And it brings me peace to think that maybe-
Maybe,

-I got the opportunity to in another.

We Were Once So Beautiful

We were once so beautiful...

A beauty so unspeakable it could only seen in
the realm of imagination.

You and I, versions of ourselves, described in
the highest form of purity.

I saw you, with an aura so gravitational, it could
only be described the way the sea pulls the sand.

The way your presence pulled me deeper; I was
lost in your essence and everything that was you.

But as summer turns to winter,
The weather becomes colder
And so did we.

Silence turned to shatters echoing in our
thoughts.

Your words thrown like daggers to my soul

And I, I spoke emptiness into existence

Vicious tongue with venomous bites,

Lingering in your mind and following you like
your shadow in the light.

There is no place to hide.

A shelter that once stood tall is now an array of
ashes and residue from the bombs we used to
destroy each other.

And there you are, a silhouette of the portrait of
love I once painted across the stars...

A mirror image of uncertainty reflecting from
the water running down my cheek in the shape
of a tear.

And there I am,

Watering a plant, in hopes a flower may bloom
in the dark.

Loose Change

1. I am often stuck spending time scraping the
remnants of love from the bottom of my feet and
the tips of my fingers and the very top of my
head just to have enough for everyone.
Maybe I have hidden some in the couch
cushions for safekeeping.
I shall check soon.

2. It is hardly enough to have love. You must
know how to utilize it properly. Otherwise - it
will wiggle its way into the cracks; expand and
contract, until something breaks – lost forever.
So much of my heart is directionless. Perhaps I
am a poet merely because all of my drawers are
mislabeled. And, thus, my intentions are
disorganized. Pity.

3. I sit here quietly as the walls crack and
crumble, falling gracefully onto a floor that is
weathered with old disasters that have been
hurriedly buffed and polished to look
presentable. I will wait here until the symphony
of catastrophe quiets and the next chapter's
sunny, short overture begins.

Hopefully the stores will have cleaning supplies by then.

Weeds

I am the dandelion
And you are the wind.

I am stuck
Here
In our kismet back and forth

Between all I can give to you
And all you can take

Weed is a slur to me.

Though my petals still ripen to
A honey hue of
Sunshine-

Occasionally-
I catch the nervous glimpse
of a Rose's admirer peer my way.

It must have been embarrassing
To choose me
Over her

And get caught.

Her with her rouge tint
And opulent curvature;
- A florists' climactic summit

Me with
my sharp edges
And humble foundations
- Dad's 'least fucked up' child

-

There is hope and then
There is blindness

I am still considering which is truth.

The drunk and powerless mind: a ticker-tape of thought

1. Sometimes I'm scared that you already had your great love story

2. I wish I had a never ending triscuit box.

3. "Transactional friendships"

4. It disgusts me to think of sleeping with a watch on.

5. Bathtub in the living room

6. The person who has the power in the relationship is the one who loves the least.

7. 12:32 - lights went out.

8. "I am me despite you."

9. Socks and batteries

10. I don't think I'm the firework; only the spectator.

11. "It has to be someone I can see heaven through."

12. Portland Texas- hotel smelled like almost-cinnamon buns.

13. Hot and perfumed nature.

14. Cicadas.

15. Escape the fire, Z.

River of Lethe

I will keep you safe-
Under the rapids of long dark
Waves.

I will hold your heart
As Medusa's long lost kin-
-cradled close to the nucleus of
Me.

No one exists under the dusty, powder fragrance
of
pillow tousled hair

Except me.
Except you.

The ugly parts-
split ends and greying roots
Veil us with a spirit of play;

Painting our faces with
The color of passion-
And compassion-
And-

The architecture of
A dying king's final smile.

we are both young again.

Through the brambles of mornings
And late nights-
And poorly made drinks.

But I promise,

I will keep you safe-
Under the rapids of long dark
Waves.

For as long as I can

Sometimes

Sometimes it's scares me-
Our cities

Where our former selves called home;
Where the people we were in another life-
Stuck their souls and never let go.

Back ache

Pick me up off the floor
I have walked too long

I'm not tired
No
But I want you to carry my inanimate weight

Just once

Love,

Sweet Magnolia,

Treat me like I cannot survive

Baby,

My baby,

Don't let me spare
Even one
iota of energy

Show me
You'll live
So that I don't have to.

Push my lungs
With both hands

Gently
Through time

Show me you'll keep me alive.

Veuve Clicquot

I admired you like you were an old note
Hidden in a pocket;

Forgotten for years
-Our sacred covenant of juvenile ramblings-

always accidentally brought up in dimly lit bar
rooms
-Speaking of the 'good ol days'
(were they?)

"Oh I remember him"
I say nonchalantly
To people I don't really know.

The conversation usually stopped there-

But my old jeans
That haven't looked the same on me
Since your pressure changed the ridges of
my hips
(Do you think of that day too?)

Are igniting in the back of my childhood
Closet-
With a smoldering resistance

It echos:

I will not be forgotten
I will survive
Somewhere in the recesses of your ocean heart

Love is intrepid -

Until it is salted
And burned.

But I don't live in that old farmhouse anymore
And that new couple
Who got a great deal
On their first nest-

Has never found my old bell-bottoms.

Excalibur

I have work in a good 6 hours-

Am I real
Or transparent?

Is everything I'm doing worthwhile

Or am I just a throw pillow
In the scheme of life

I'm exhausted all the time-

Unless I am writing;

Then-
I am invincible

The pen is my savior
I shall not want.

Kin

I thought I understood it, but I didn't.
I am standing here with a blown-out red candle.

I thought I gave you enough.
I thought we all lost enough.

But maybe history was written wrong

I thought you loved me
I guess sister is just a fancy word for,
"similar."

I have seen death, just like you.
I have lived for you.

When you look back at the tragedies,
tell me -
who was it that you were crying on?

Who was it that looked the other way?

You don't have to answer
-although you know.

So,
This is a letter to you.
The upsetting you.
This is a letter to the bad you.
- the only type of you.
This is all about you.

The you that dissolved my heart.
The you that has set alight all of our home
movies.
The you that made me invisible-
a loveless husk of a human.

This is a letter to you, you devine
disappointment.

This is my letter to inform you-
That your membership will not renew.

I will become your ghost
And you will one day wonder if you only
invented the thought of me

I will sing so loudly
everyday
that life itself will dance with me.

You will slowly recede into my lonely, wearied
past
with all the rest-

In the catacombs of my forgetfulness;
In the abyss of the sea around us all.

I am baptized once more-

I thought I understood it, but I didn't.
I was yellow in a field of grey.
Now I know,
That this was my power.

Halon

I lit a candle and wandered away
Who trusted her waxing tears?
The shadows of infidelity play.

Before I left, I thought to stay-
But betrayal convinced me rare-
So I lit a candle and wandered away.

Secrets told through inferno prey.
The eyes of the ash do not but glare.
The shadows of infidelity play.

A confidant waits for the waning day.
The moon decides what's fair.
I lit a candle and wandered away.

Falsity tends to keep demons at bay.
Sometimes the flames do care!
The shadows of infidelity play.

It's the wind; He holds the final say.
For the wicked, her bed is prepared.
I lit a candle and wandered away.
I let the shadows of infidelity play.

Laurel and Jena

My apologies for saying

I love you.
-          How naive can Yankees be?
Though, if by chance,
It wasn't love-

It certainly was
-          Something wonderful
Something like a fleur-de-lis
Something like his morning breath
-          Or the smile that happened to sweeten it.
Something like driving away
-          Or perhaps floating
Something like May Rain,
Or the beers we never finished under the covers;
-          Too busy feeling around each other's
darkness for a light switch
Something about bare feet-
And dirty sidewalks.

Who knew I'd miss you so
Suddenly
Swiftly
Slowly

I wonder if the bandanas
Helped you see me better-

Through the cloudy make up of a stranger
-          Into the warm embrace of a confidant

Something about the land
-          And how it pushed us
Where laughter grew
To be harvested bountifully
And I sometimes think-
We were the alligators
We so frivolously searched for;

Elusive
Aggressive
Powerfully aware of one another

I haven't written in 6 months.
Allow me to say thank you-
For showing me where the pen hides in my
mind.
-          Deep beneath the floorboards and beads
On Laurel
I guess this is just-
A little something wonderful.
A little something about sharing the mood.
A little something like you.
A little something like who we were that week.

And if it wasn't love
-it must've just been New Orleans.